EMMANUEL JOSEPH

The Currency of Vision, How Billionaires Turn Dreams into Global Legacies

Copyright © 2025 by Emmanuel Joseph

All rights reserved. No part of this publication may be reproduced, stored or transmitted in any form or by any means, electronic, mechanical, photocopying, recording, scanning, or otherwise without written permission from the publisher. It is illegal to copy this book, post it to a website, or distribute it by any other means without permission.

First edition

This book was professionally typeset on Reedsy. Find out more at reedsy.com

Contents

1	Chapter 1: The Power of Vision	1
2	Chapter 2: Dream to Plan	2
3	Chapter 3: Risk and Reward	3
4	Chapter 4: Cultivating Innovation	4
5	Chapter 5: Building a Stellar Team	5
6	Chapter 6: Resilience in Adversity	6
7	Chapter 7: Strategic Partnerships	7
8	Chapter 8: Embracing Technology	8
9	Chapter 9: Financial Mastery	9
10	Chapter 10: Social Responsibility	10
11	Chapter 11: Adapting to Change	11
12	Chapter 12: Creating a Brand Identity	12
13	Chapter 13: Long-Term Thinking	13
14	Chapter 14: Empowering Others	14
15	Chapter 15: Leveraging Media and Communication	15
16	Chapter 16: Legacy Planning and Succession	16
17	Chapter 17: The Currency of Vision	18

1

Chapter 1: The Power of Vision

Every great legacy begins with a clear and compelling vision. For billionaires like Elon Musk and Jeff Bezos, their visions are not just dreams—they are blueprints for the future. Elon Musk's vision of a multi-planetary human existence drives his endeavors with SpaceX, while Jeff Bezos' dream of an interconnected global marketplace propelled Amazon to unprecedented heights. Their visions act as a compass, guiding every decision and strategy, no matter how challenging the path may be.

A compelling vision is more than an abstract idea; it's a detailed picture of the future. Musk's vision includes colonizing Mars and making space travel affordable for everyone. Bezos envisioned a world where consumers could buy anything online with just a few clicks. These visions are not confined by the limitations of the present but instead boldly imagine what could be possible.

The power of a vision lies in its ability to inspire and mobilize. Musk and Bezos have not only set their sights on grand goals but have also inspired countless individuals to join them on their journeys. Their visions resonate with employees, investors, and customers alike, creating a shared sense of purpose and driving collective efforts towards a common goal.

In essence, the first step to turning dreams into a global legacy is to craft a vision so compelling that it transcends the boundaries of imagination and inspires others to believe in its possibility.

2

Chapter 2: Dream to Plan

Having a vision is only the first step. The transition from dreaming to planning is where the magic truly begins. Successful billionaires like Bill Gates and Warren Buffett exemplify this process. Gates' vision of a computer on every desk in every home required meticulous planning, from software development to market penetration strategies. Buffett's vision of building a diversified investment portfolio led him to create detailed financial roadmaps and investment strategies.

Planning involves breaking down the grand vision into manageable steps and setting clear milestones. Gates' approach to developing Microsoft Windows included setting specific goals for each version, ensuring continuous improvement and innovation. Buffett's investment philosophy revolves around detailed analysis and long-term planning, ensuring sustained growth and success.

A well-structured plan serves as a roadmap, guiding every action and decision. It helps visionaries stay focused and navigate the complexities of implementation. Gates and Buffett's ability to convert their dreams into actionable blueprints has been a key factor in their success, enabling them to turn visionary ideas into concrete realities.

In summary, the bridge between a dream and its realization is a meticulously crafted plan that outlines the path to achieving the envisioned future.

3

Chapter 3: Risk and Reward

With great dreams come great risks. Visionary billionaires like Richard Branson and Oprah Winfrey understand that taking bold risks is an integral part of turning dreams into reality. Branson's ventures into various industries, from airlines to space tourism, exemplify his willingness to embrace uncertainty and challenge the status quo. Oprah's decision to launch her own television network was a significant gamble, driven by her belief in the power of storytelling and positive impact.

Risk-taking involves stepping into the unknown and facing potential failure head-on. Branson's journey with Virgin Galactic has been fraught with challenges, yet his unwavering commitment to making space travel accessible has kept him pushing forward. Oprah's network faced initial struggles, but her resilience and dedication to her vision eventually led to its success.

The rewards of taking calculated risks can be transformative. Branson's ventures have not only disrupted industries but also inspired innovation and competition. Oprah's network has provided a platform for diverse voices and stories, amplifying her impact on media and culture. Their stories demonstrate that risk-taking is not just about seeking profit but about making a meaningful difference.

In conclusion, the willingness to take bold risks and navigate uncertainty is a hallmark of visionary leaders who turn their dreams into global legacies.

4

Chapter 4: Cultivating Innovation

Innovation is the lifeblood of legacy-building. Visionaries like Steve Jobs and Larry Page understand that fostering a culture of innovation within their organizations is crucial for sustained success. Jobs' relentless pursuit of perfection and Page's experimental approach at Google have led to groundbreaking advancements that have reshaped entire industries.

Cultivating innovation involves creating an environment where creativity and experimentation are encouraged. Jobs' emphasis on design and user experience drove Apple's innovative products, from the iPod to the iPhone. Page's philosophy of "moonshot thinking" at Google encourages employees to tackle ambitious projects that have the potential to change the world.

Innovation is not just about developing new products; it's about reimagining how things are done. Jobs' focus on simplicity and elegance in design revolutionized consumer electronics. Page's commitment to data-driven decision-making and continuous improvement has kept Google at the forefront of technological innovation.

In essence, the ability to cultivate innovation within an organization is a key factor in building a lasting legacy. Visionaries who embrace creativity and foster a culture of innovation drive progress and create enduring impact.

5

Chapter 5: Building a Stellar Team

No visionary can succeed alone. The importance of assembling a talented and dedicated team cannot be overstated. Howard Schultz, the man behind Starbucks, and Sheryl Sandberg, COO of Facebook, are prime examples of leaders who understand the power of a strong support system.

Schultz recognized early on that creating a welcoming and consistent coffee experience required a team that was equally passionate about the mission. By investing in employee training and fostering a sense of ownership among staff, Schultz built a team that was committed to delivering the Starbucks experience. Similarly, Sandberg's leadership at Facebook has been characterized by her ability to attract and retain top talent, driving the company's growth and innovation.

Effective team-building involves more than just hiring the right people; it's about creating an environment where team members feel valued and empowered. Schultz's emphasis on treating employees with respect and providing opportunities for growth has resulted in a loyal and motivated workforce. Sandberg's focus on mentorship and collaboration has cultivated a culture of continuous improvement and shared success.

In summary, building a stellar team is a crucial element in turning visionary dreams into reality. A dedicated and talented team can amplify the impact of a visionary leader and help transform ambitious goals into lasting legacies.

6

Chapter 6: Resilience in Adversity

Challenges are inevitable on the path to legacy. The resilience and determination of visionaries like Jack Ma, founder of Alibaba, and Sara Blakely, founder of Spanx, are testaments to the power of perseverance.

Jack Ma's journey is marked by numerous rejections and setbacks. From being turned down for jobs to facing skepticism from investors, Ma encountered countless obstacles. However, his unwavering belief in his vision for Alibaba kept him pushing forward. Today, Alibaba is one of the world's largest e-commerce companies, a testament to Ma's resilience.

Sara Blakely's story is equally inspiring. She started Spanx with just $5,000 in savings, facing rejection from manufacturers and skepticism from industry experts. Blakely's determination and innovative approach to shapewear eventually led to Spanx becoming a global phenomenon. Her story underscores the importance of persistence and resilience in overcoming challenges and achieving success.

In conclusion, resilience in the face of adversity is a defining trait of visionary leaders. Their ability to navigate setbacks and use challenges as opportunities for growth is key to building enduring legacies.

7

Chapter 7: Strategic Partnerships

Partnerships can amplify a visionary's impact and open new avenues for achieving grand visions. Billionaires like Mark Zuckerberg and Larry Ellison have leveraged strategic alliances to expand their influence and drive innovation.

Mark Zuckerberg's collaboration with Sheryl Sandberg brought invaluable expertise to Facebook, guiding its growth and monetization strategies. Sandberg's experience in advertising and her leadership skills complemented Zuckerberg's technical acumen, resulting in a powerful partnership that propelled Facebook to new heights.

Larry Ellison, co-founder of Oracle, has also utilized strategic partnerships to strengthen his company's position in the technology industry. Ellison's collaboration with other tech giants and his focus on acquisitions have enabled Oracle to stay competitive and continuously innovate.

Strategic partnerships involve identifying complementary strengths and working together towards common goals. Zuckerberg and Ellison's ability to forge strong alliances has been instrumental in their success, demonstrating that collaboration can be a powerful tool for achieving visionary dreams.

In summary, the ability to build and maintain strategic partnerships is a critical factor in turning visionary ideas into global legacies. Partnerships can provide new perspectives, resources, and opportunities for growth, enhancing the impact of visionary leaders.

8

Chapter 8: Embracing Technology

Technology is a powerful tool for realizing visionary dreams. Visionaries like Elon Musk and Jeff Bezos have harnessed the potential of cutting-edge technology to drive progress and create transformative impact.

Elon Musk's ventures, from SpaceX to Tesla, are driven by his commitment to technological innovation. SpaceX's advancements in reusable rockets and Tesla's breakthroughs in electric vehicles are examples of how Musk leverages technology to achieve his vision of a sustainable and interconnected future.

Jeff Bezos' vision for Amazon was built on the foundation of technological innovation. From the early days of e-commerce to the development of cloud computing with Amazon Web Services (AWS), Bezos has consistently embraced technology to stay ahead of the curve and deliver unparalleled value to customers.

The ability to integrate and adapt to new technologies is essential for visionary leaders. Musk and Bezos' willingness to invest in research and development, experiment with new ideas, and push the boundaries of what is possible has been key to their success.

In essence, embracing technology is a critical component of turning visionary dreams into reality. Visionaries who leverage technological advancements can drive innovation, improve efficiency, and create lasting impact.

Chapter 9: Financial Mastery

Financial acumen is crucial for sustaining and expanding a vision. Billionaires like Warren Buffett and George Soros have mastered the art of financial management, using their expertise to build and maintain their legacies. Buffett's investment strategies, grounded in value investing, have turned Berkshire Hathaway into one of the most successful conglomerates in the world. His ability to analyze companies and make informed decisions has been key to his long-term success.

George Soros, on the other hand, has leveraged his understanding of financial markets to create substantial wealth and influence. His ability to predict market trends and take calculated risks has resulted in significant returns. Soros' financial mastery extends beyond personal wealth; his philanthropic efforts through the Open Society Foundations have had a profound impact on global issues.

Financial mastery involves more than just generating wealth; it's about managing resources effectively and ensuring the longevity of a vision. Buffett and Soros' disciplined approaches to financial management and their commitment to giving back illustrate how financial acumen can turn visionary dreams into lasting legacies.

10

Chapter 10: Social Responsibility

True legacies are built on more than just financial success. Social responsibility and giving back to the community are integral components of a visionary's journey. Billionaires like Bill Gates and Melinda French Gates exemplify this principle through their philanthropic efforts.

The Bill & Melinda Gates Foundation, one of the largest private foundations in the world, focuses on global health, education, and poverty alleviation. Bill and Melinda's commitment to addressing pressing social issues has made a significant impact, from eradicating diseases to improving access to education. Their approach to philanthropy is driven by data and evidence, ensuring that their contributions have a meaningful and lasting effect.

Social responsibility involves recognizing the broader impact of one's actions and using resources to make a positive difference. Gates' dedication to philanthropy and his belief in the power of collective action demonstrate that a commitment to social causes enriches and solidifies a visionary's legacy.

In conclusion, embracing social responsibility is a vital element of building a legacy. Visionaries who prioritize giving back create a ripple effect that extends far beyond their immediate sphere of influence.

11

Chapter 11: Adapting to Change

Change is constant, and adaptability is essential for sustaining a legacy. Visionaries like Jeff Bezos and Elon Musk have demonstrated remarkable flexibility in navigating evolving landscapes and seizing new opportunities.

Jeff Bezos' ability to pivot and innovate has been a driving force behind Amazon's continued success. From expanding into cloud computing with AWS to venturing into entertainment with Amazon Prime Video, Bezos' willingness to embrace change has kept Amazon at the forefront of multiple industries. His focus on customer-centric innovation and long-term thinking has allowed Amazon to adapt and thrive in an ever-changing market.

Elon Musk's ventures, including Tesla and SpaceX, are built on a foundation of adaptability and forward-thinking. Musk's commitment to continuous improvement and his readiness to tackle new challenges have driven technological advancements and reshaped entire industries. His ability to pivot when faced with obstacles and explore uncharted territories has been key to his success.

In essence, the ability to adapt to change and remain flexible is a defining trait of visionary leaders. Their willingness to embrace uncertainty and navigate evolving landscapes ensures that their legacies endure and continue to make an impact.

12

Chapter 12: Creating a Brand Identity

A strong brand identity is a cornerstone of a lasting legacy. Visionaries like Steve Jobs and Richard Branson understand the power of branding and have crafted compelling narratives around their brands.

Steve Jobs' meticulous attention to detail and his emphasis on design and user experience have defined Apple's brand identity. Apple's products, from the iPhone to the MacBook, are synonymous with innovation, elegance, and simplicity. Jobs' ability to create a brand that resonates with customers on an emotional level has been instrumental in building Apple's global legacy.

Richard Branson's Virgin brand is characterized by its adventurous spirit and commitment to customer satisfaction. From airlines to music, the Virgin brand represents quality, innovation, and a sense of fun. Branson's focus on creating a distinctive and relatable brand identity has allowed Virgin to expand into diverse industries while maintaining its core values.

In summary, creating a strong brand identity involves crafting a narrative that reflects the vision and values of a company. Visionaries who prioritize branding ensure that their message resonates with audiences worldwide, leaving a lasting impression.

13

Chapter 13: Long-Term Thinking

Visionaries think beyond immediate gains. The long-term thinking and planning of billionaires like Elon Musk and Jeff Bezos have been crucial in achieving their grand visions. Musk's focus on sustainable energy and space exploration reflects his commitment to solving long-term global challenges. Tesla's mission to accelerate the world's transition to sustainable energy and SpaceX's goal of making life multi-planetary are both driven by a long-term perspective.

Jeff Bezos' approach to Amazon's growth has always been rooted in long-term thinking. From reinvesting profits into the business to continually expanding into new markets, Bezos prioritizes sustainable growth over short-term gains. His emphasis on customer-centric innovation and long-term planning has positioned Amazon as a global leader in e-commerce and technology.

Long-term thinking involves setting ambitious goals and being patient enough to see them through. Musk and Bezos' ability to maintain a forward-thinking mindset and prioritize future impact ensures that their legacies endure and continue to make a difference.

In essence, visionary leaders who think long-term create a lasting impact that extends far beyond their immediate successes.

Chapter 14: Empowering Others

Empowering others is a key component of a visionary's legacy. Billionaires like Oprah Winfrey and Howard Schultz understand the importance of inspiring and uplifting those around them. Oprah's commitment to empowerment is evident in her media empire, which focuses on positive storytelling and personal growth. Through her talk show, magazine, and television network, Oprah has created platforms for diverse voices and encouraged millions to pursue their dreams.

Howard Schultz's leadership at Starbucks is characterized by his dedication to creating opportunities for employees. Schultz's emphasis on treating employees with respect and providing benefits such as healthcare and education assistance has fostered a culture of empowerment. By investing in his team and creating a supportive work environment, Schultz has built a loyal and motivated workforce.

Empowering others involves recognizing and nurturing potential, providing opportunities for growth, and inspiring confidence. Oprah and Schultz's commitment to empowerment extends their influence and impact, creating a ripple effect that reaches far beyond their immediate spheres.

In conclusion, visionary leaders who prioritize empowering others build a legacy that is not only successful but also meaningful and transformative.

15

Chapter 15: Leveraging Media and Communication

Effective communication amplifies a visionary's message. Billionaires like Mark Zuckerberg and Sheryl Sandberg understand the power of media and communication in spreading their visions and building lasting legacies. Zuckerberg's creation of Facebook revolutionized the way people connect and share information. His ability to leverage social media to reach a global audience has transformed communication and created a platform for diverse voices and perspectives.

Sheryl Sandberg's expertise in communication has been instrumental in Facebook's growth and success. Her focus on clear and transparent communication, both internally and externally, has helped build trust and credibility. Sandberg's initiatives, such as Lean In, have also empowered individuals to share their stories and advocate for gender equality.

Leveraging media and communication involves crafting a compelling narrative and using various platforms to spread the message. Zuckerberg and Sandberg's ability to harness the power of storytelling and connect with audiences has been key to their success.

In summary, effective communication is a crucial element in building a lasting legacy. Visionaries who leverage media and communication to amplify their message can reach a wider audience and create a more significant impact.

16

Chapter 16: Legacy Planning and Succession

Planning for the future is crucial for sustaining a legacy. Billionaires like Warren Buffett and Larry Page understand the importance of succession planning and ensuring their visions continue to thrive beyond their leadership. Buffett's approach to succession planning at Berkshire Hathaway involves identifying and mentoring talented individuals who can carry forward his vision. His emphasis on a seamless transition and maintaining the company's values ensures that Berkshire Hathaway remains successful and impactful.

Larry Page's focus on innovation and long-term thinking at Google has also involved careful succession planning. By appointing Sundar Pichai as CEO, Page ensured that Google's vision of continuous improvement and technological advancement would be maintained. Pichai's leadership has kept Google at the forefront of innovation while preserving the company's core values.

Legacy planning and succession involve preparing for the future and ensuring that the vision and values of the organization are upheld. Buffett and Page's commitment to thoughtful succession planning ensures that their legacies continue to thrive and make a difference.

In essence, visionary leaders who prioritize legacy planning and succession creat a lasting impact that extends far beyond their tenure.

17

Chapter 17: The Currency of Vision

In the final chapter, we tie together all the elements discussed in the book. Visionaries like Elon Musk, Jeff Bezos, Oprah Winfrey, and Warren Buffett have demonstrated that the true currency of vision lies in its ability to inspire, innovate, and create lasting impact. Their journeys are a testament to the power of a clear and compelling vision, meticulous planning, bold risk-taking, and a commitment to empowering others.

By examining the collective lessons from the lives of these billionaires, we see that turning dreams into global legacies requires more than just financial success. It involves a combination of vision, innovation, resilience, and social responsibility. Visionaries who embrace these principles create a ripple effect that extends far beyond their immediate successes, leaving a lasting legacy that inspires and transforms the world.

In conclusion, the currency of vision is not measured in dollars or assets but in the enduring impact and positive change that visionary leaders create. Their legacies serve as a reminder that with a clear vision and unwavering dedication, dreams can indeed become global legacies.

The Currency of Vision: How Billionaires Turn Dreams into Global Legacies

In "The Currency of Vision," journey into the minds of the world's most influential billionaires and discover the secrets behind their enduring legacies. This book delves into the pivotal elements that transform visionary dreams

CHAPTER 17: THE CURRENCY OF VISION

into global realities, exploring the journeys of icons like Elon Musk, Jeff Bezos, Oprah Winfrey, and Warren Buffett.

Each chapter unveils a crucial aspect of their success, from the power of a compelling vision and meticulous planning to the bold risks that fuel innovation. Learn how they build stellar teams, navigate adversity with resilience, and forge strategic partnerships that amplify their impact.

Understand the importance of embracing technology, mastering financial strategies, and prioritizing social responsibility. Discover how these visionaries adapt to change, create strong brand identities, and think long-term to ensure their legacies endure.

"The Currency of Vision" also highlights the significance of empowering others, leveraging media and communication, and planning for succession. Through captivating anecdotes and insights, this book reveals that the true currency of vision lies in its ability to inspire, innovate, and create lasting impact.

Whether you're an aspiring entrepreneur, a seasoned leader, or simply curious about the minds of the world's greatest visionaries, this book offers invaluable lessons on turning dreams into legacies that shape the world.

www.ingramcontent.com/pod-product-compliance
Lightning Source LLC
LaVergne TN
LVHW010446070526
838199LV00066B/6223